USING
MATHS
SURVIVAL SKILLS

by Hilary Koll, Steve Mills
and Jonny Crockett

ticktock

USING
MATHS
SURVIVAL SKILLS

Copyright © ticktock Entertainment Ltd 2006
First published in Great Britain in 2006 by ticktock Media Ltd.,
The Old Sawmill, 103 Goods Station Road, Tunbridge Wells, Kent, TN1 2DP
ISBN 978 1 86007 990 0
Printed in China
9 8 7 6 5 4 3 2

HILARY KOLL

Hilary Koll (B.Ed. Hons) was a Leading Maths Teacher in a primary school before training as a Numeracy Consultant for the National Numeracy Strategy. She has worked as a Lecturer in Mathematics Education at the University of Reading, teaching on undergraduate, post-graduate and training courses. She is now a full-time writer and consultant in mathematics education. Hilary Koll and Steve Mills can be contacted via their website www.cmeprojects.com

STEVE MILLS

Steve Mills (B.A. Hons, P.G.C.E., M.Ed.) was a teacher of both primary and secondary age children and an LEA Maths Advisory Support Teacher before joining the University of Reading as a Lecturer in Mathematics Education. He worked with both under-graduate and post-graduate students in their preparation for teaching maths in schools. He has written many mathematics books for both teachers and children. Visit www.cmeprojects.com for details.

JONNY CROCKETT

Jonny went on his first survival course when he was 14 years old. Since then, he has travelled all over the world to learn the skills and techniques that are still used by some people as a way of life. In 1997 Jonny established the Survival School in Exeter to share his enthusiasm for bushcraft. He now runs courses in locations from the Sahara Desert to the Jungles of Borneo. You can see more about Survival School at www.survivalschool.co.uk

CONTENTS

NUMERACY WORK COVERED IN THIS BOOK:

CALCULATIONS:
Throughout this book there are opportunities to practise **addition, subtraction, multiplication** and **division** using both mental calculation strategies and pencil and paper methods.

NUMBERS AND THE NUMBER SYSTEM:
- 12 x TABLE: pg. 16
- COMPARING & ORDERING NUMBERS: pgs. 12, 14, 18
- ESTIMATING: pgs. 6, 7, 12
- FRACTIONS: pgs. 13, 18, 24
- ROUNDING NUMBERS: pg. 14

SOLVING 'REAL LIFE' PROBLEMS:
- CHOOSING THE OPERATION: pgs. 7, 12, 20, 21
- MAPS: pgs. 9, 11
- MEASURES: pg. 18
- PROBABILITY: pgs. 24, 25
- TIME: pgs. 12, 13, 22, 23

HANDLING DATA:
- PICTOGRAMS: pg. 21
- USING TABLES/CHARTS/DIAGRAMS: pgs. 6, 7

MEASURES:
- PERIMETER: pg. 16
- RELATIONSHIPS BETWEEN UNITS OF MEASUREMENT: pgs. 14, 18

SHAPE AND SPACE:
- 2-D SHAPES: pgs. 12, 16
- 3-D SHAPES: pg. 17
- ANGLES: pgs. 8, 9
- COMPASS DIRECTIONS: pgs. 8, 9, 10, 11
- GRID CO-ORDINATES: pgs. 10, 11

Supports the maths work taught at Key Stage 2 and 3

HOW TO USE THIS BOOK

Maths is important in the lives of people everywhere. We use maths when we play a game, ride a bike, go shopping – in fact, all the time! Everyone needs to use maths at work. You may not realise it, but a survival expert would use maths to live in the wild! With this book you will get the chance to try lots of exciting maths activities using real life data and facts about survival situations. Practise your maths and numeracy skills and experience the thrill of what it's really like to pit your wits against the great outdoors.

This exciting maths book is very easy to use – check out what's inside!

Fun to read information about how to survive if you find yourself stranded in the wilderness.

MATHS ACTIVITIES

Look for the
SURVIVAL SKILLS WORK.
You will find real life maths
activities and questions to try.

To answer some of the questions,
you will need to collect data from
a DATA BOX. Sometimes, you will
need to collect facts and data
from the text or from charts
and diagrams.

Be prepared! You will need a pen
or pencil and a notebook for your
workings and answers.

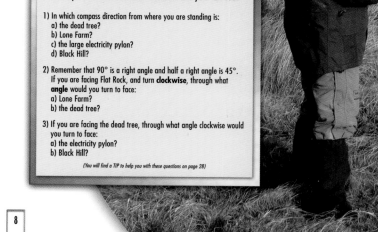

NAVIGATION – USE A COMPASS

You have gone for a walk in the countryside with three friends. After you have stopped for lunch you look around and realize that you are not sure where you are. You see a church in the distance and use your **compass** to work out that it is directly to the North of you. There is only one picnic site marked on the map which has a church to the North. You check this position is correct by looking at other landmarks. As you look around you, you can see an electricity **pylon** and a farm building. There is a hill in the distance and a rocky outcrop with a flat top. You've found the right spot on your map. Now you need to decide where to go next.

SURVIVAL SKILLS WORK

In the DATA BOX on page 9 you will see a sketch of the surrounding countryside. From where you are standing, the picnic site, you can see the church spire directly North from you. There are other features that you can see.

1) In which compass direction from where you are standing is:
   a) the dead tree?
   b) Lone Farm?
   c) the large electricity pylon?
   d) Black Hill?

2) Remember that 90° is a right angle and half a right angle is 45°. If you are facing Flat Rock, and turn **clockwise**, through what **angle** would you turn to face:
   a) Lone Farm?
   b) the dead tree?

3) If you are facing the dead tree, through what angle clockwise would you turn to face:
   a) the electricity pylon?
   b) Black Hill?

(You will find a TIP to help you with these questions on page 28)

DATA BOX

If you see one of these boxes, there will be important data inside that will help you with the maths activities.

MATHS ACTIVITIES

Feeling confident? Try these extra **CHALLENGE QUESTIONS.**

IF YOU NEED HELP...

TIPS FOR MATHS SUCCESS

On pages 28 – 29 you will find lots of tips to help you with your maths work.

ANSWERS

Turn to pages 30 – 31 to check your answers.
(Try all the activities and questions before you take a look at the answers.)

GLOSSARY

On page 32 there is a glossary of survival words and a glossary of maths words. The glossary words appear **in bold** in the text.

DATA BOX — MAP OF THE AREA

Church
Electricity Pylon
Flat Rock
Black Hill
Picnic Site
Lone Farm
YOU ARE HERE
Dead Tree

N
NW   NE
W   E
SW   SE
S

CHALLENGE QUESTION

1) You face Black Hill and turn 135° clockwise. What do you turn to face?
2) You face the electricity pylon and turn 270° **anticlockwise.** What do you turn to face?
3) You face Lone Farm and turn 225° clockwise. What do you turn to face?

SURVIVAL FACTS

Compass needles always point to **magnetic North**, but magnetic North is in a slightly different direction from place to place and year to year.

The difference between magnetic North and North on a map (**geographic north**) is called magnetic variation.

A map and a compass will help you to find the right direction.

9

Fun to read facts and tips to help you cope in a survival situation.

SURVIVAL KIT

Survival means 'remaining alive' and there are many situations that humans can find themselves in where survival isn't easy! In our modern world we have warm homes, electric fires, food from the supermarket and plenty of running water, but what if you found yourself lost in a forest? How would you survive? To survive, humans need four main things: shelter, warmth, food and clean water. We need shelter and warmth to protect us from the rain and cold, and food and water to keep our bodies working properly. What would you eat in a forest? Where would you find clean water? How would you make a shelter? What are the basic things that could help keep you alive?

SURVIVAL SKILLS WORK

In the DATA BOX on page 7 you will see the 10 most important items to have in a survival kit. They are listed in order of importance, the first being the most important and the last being least important. Which of these following kits do you think will be most useful in saving your life?

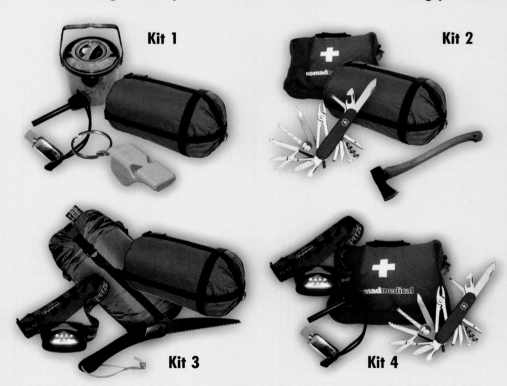

To help you decide, points have been given to each of the items. Use the points to help you find out which of the kits is worth the most points and would be most useful.

(You will find a TIP to help you with these questions on page 28)

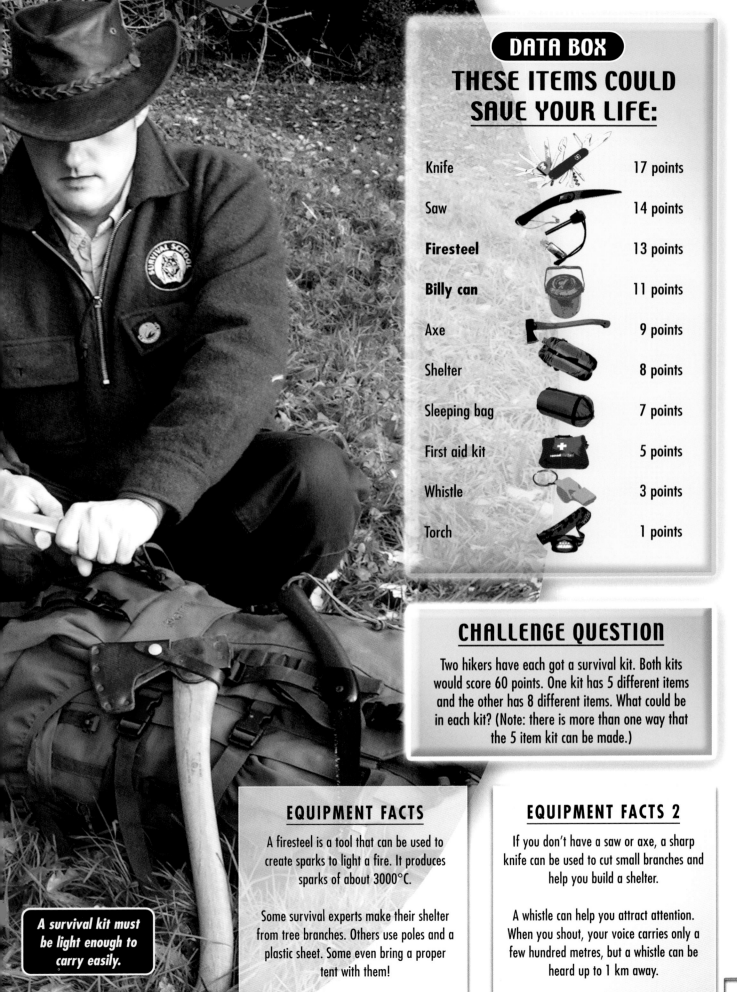

DATA BOX

THESE ITEMS COULD SAVE YOUR LIFE:

Knife		17 points
Saw		14 points
Firesteel		13 points
Billy can		11 points
Axe		9 points
Shelter		8 points
Sleeping bag		7 points
First aid kit		5 points
Whistle		3 points
Torch		1 points

CHALLENGE QUESTION

Two hikers have each got a survival kit. Both kits would score 60 points. One kit has 5 different items and the other has 8 different items. What could be in each kit? (Note: there is more than one way that the 5 item kit can be made.)

EQUIPMENT FACTS

A firesteel is a tool that can be used to create sparks to light a fire. It produces sparks of about 3000°C.

Some survival experts make their shelter from tree branches. Others use poles and a plastic sheet. Some even bring a proper tent with them!

EQUIPMENT FACTS 2

If you don't have a saw or axe, a sharp knife can be used to cut small branches and help you build a shelter.

A whistle can help you attract attention. When you shout, your voice carries only a few hundred metres, but a whistle can be heard up to 1 km away.

A survival kit must be light enough to carry easily.

NAVIGATION – USE A COMPASS

You have gone for a walk in the countryside with three friends. After you have stopped for lunch you look around and realize that you are not sure where you are. You see a church in the distance and use your **compass** to work out that it is directly to the North of you. There is only one picnic site marked on the map which has a church to the North. You check this position is correct by looking at other landmarks. As you look around you, you can see an electricity **pylon** and a farm building. There is a hill in the distance and a rocky outcrop with a flat top. You've found the right spot on your map. Now you need to decide where to go next.

SURVIVAL SKILLS WORK

In the DATA BOX on page 9 you will see a sketch of the surrounding countryside. From where you are standing, the picnic site, you can see the church spire directly North from you. There are other features that you can see.

1) In which compass direction from where you are standing is:
   a) the dead tree?
   b) Lone Farm?
   c) the large electricity pylon?
   d) Black Hill?

2) Remember that 90° is a right angle and half a right angle is 45°. If you are facing Flat Rock, and turn **clockwise**, through what **angle** will you turn to face:
   a) Lone Farm?
   b) the dead tree?

3) If you are facing the dead tree, through what angle clockwise will you turn to face:
   a) the electricity pylon?
   b) Flat Rock?

(You will find a TIP to help you with these questions on page 28)

MAP OF THE AREA

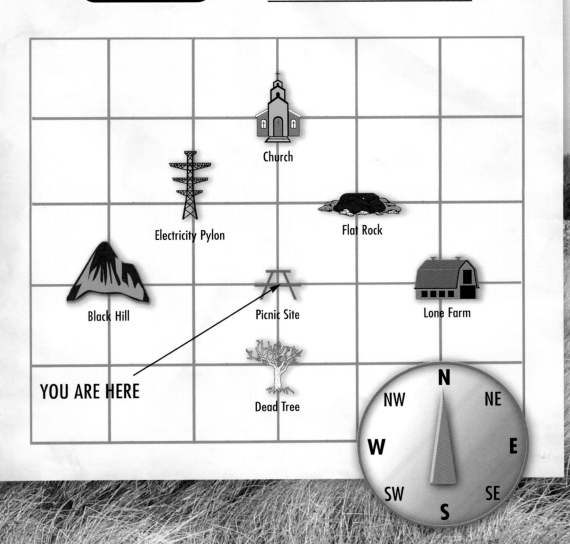

YOU ARE HERE

SURVIVAL FACTS

Compass needles always point to **magnetic North**, but magnetic North is in a slightly different direction from place to place and year to year.

The difference between magnetic North and North on a map (**geographic north**) is called magnetic variation.

A map and a compass will help you to find the right direction.

CHALLENGE QUESTION

1) You face Black Hill and turn 135° clockwise. What do you turn to face?

2) You face the electricity pylon and turn 270° **anticlockwise**. What do you turn to face?

3) You face Lone Farm and turn 225° clockwise. What do you turn to face?

NAVIGATION – USING THE SUN

Y ou and your friends set off in a South-East direction and walk for a couple of kilometres. You find yourselves deep in some woods. There are trees all around you so you need the **compass** to show you which way to go. You suddenly realize that you haven't got the compass! Someone must have dropped it back at the picnic site. Do you go all the way back to look for it? Or is there another way to find out which way to go? It is quite a sunny day, so perhaps you could use the sun! In the **Northern Hemisphere** of the world the sun is in the South at midday. In the **Southern Hemisphere** the sun is in the North at midday.

SURVIVAL SKILLS WORK

You have used the sun and your watch to work out which way is North. Look at the map in the DATA BOX on page 11. You and your friends are at the point (0, 3). Use the map to answer these questions.

1) What are the **coordinates** of each of these points on the map:
   a) Wooden Bridge?
   b) Canal Rocks?
   c) Ling Marsh?

2) What is at each of these points?
   a) (2, 0)
   b) (1, -2)
   c) (0, -3)

(You will find TIPS to help you with these questions on page 28)

CHALLENGE QUESTION

You are at (0, 0).
If you traveled in each of these directions from that point which place would you reach first:
a) E?
b) SW?
c) NW?

USING A WATCH TO FIND NORTH

If you want to work out which way is North or South you can use a watch to help you.

IF YOU ARE IN THE NORTHERN HEMISPHERE...
1) Point the hour hand of your watch towards the sun.
2) Imagine a line halfway between the hour hand and 12 on the watch. This line is a North/South line.
3) Remember that if the time is before midday, the sun will be in the East and after midday the sun will be in the West. Use this to help you work out which way is North.

IF YOU ARE IN THE SOUTHERN HEMISPHERE
1) Point 12 on your watch towards the sun.
2) Imagine a line halfway between the 12 and the hour hand to give you the North/South line.
3) Remember that if the time is before midday, the sun will be in the East and after midday the sun will be in the West. Use this to help you work out which way is North.

Northern Hemisphere

Southern Hemisphere

DATA BOX

LOOKING AT A MAP

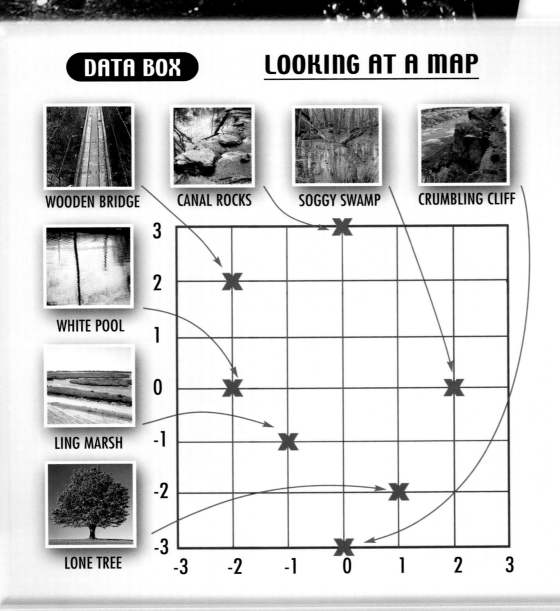

WOODEN BRIDGE CANAL ROCKS SOGGY SWAMP CRUMBLING CLIFF

WHITE POOL

LING MARSH

LONE TREE

LOST IN THE WOODS!

Unfortunately you and your friends become lost in the woods and it is getting late. You know it will be dark soon. You agree between you that it will be best to stay out overnight. You now need to plan what to do in the remaining hours of daylight so that you will survive the night. There are different things that you could choose to do; you could rest, hunt for food, build a shelter, light a fire, look for water, or gather leaves to keep you warm. You want to stay in one group and work together, so you have the time to do some of the tasks, but not all of them. Which tasks should you pick? You must decide quickly, the light is beginning to fade...

SURVIVAL SKILLS WORK

In the DATA BOX on page 13 you will see a table showing how long different jobs might take and how useful each job is in helping to keep you alive.

1) Use the information to decide which jobs you will do in the remaining 4 hours before complete darkness. Make sure that the jobs don't take more than 4 hours altogether.

2) Now find out exactly how long the jobs you decide on would take to do. Give your answer in hours and minutes.

3) How much of the 4 hours would you have to spare?

(You will find a TIP to help you with these questions on page 28)

SURVIVAL FACTS

If you survive a plane crash or a car crash in the wilderness, stay with the wreckage. It is easier to find the wreckage than it is to find one person on their own.

SURVIVAL FACTS

When you are in a survival situation you should think about fire, shelter, water and food You need to think about which is the most important for the environment you are in.

SURVIVAL FACTS

To survive, you need to be fit, have the right equipment, have the knowledge to survive and, most importantly, have a positive mental attitude.

DATA BOX   SURVIVAL TASKS

This table shows estimates of how much time each of the following jobs might take your group to complete, and how useful each task would be. Each job has been graded from 1 to 10 on how useful it will be, 10 being good and 0 being useless.

Job		Usefulness	Time it could take
Hunt for food		6	215 minutes
Build shelter		8	145 minutes
Light a fire		9	55 minutes
Look for water		7	115 minutes
Find something to keep you warm		5	150 minutes

CHALLENGE QUESTIONS

1) How much time would it take to do all of these things, in total?
   Give your answer in
   a) minutes
   b) hours and minutes

2) You do two of these jobs, and it takes 5½ hours.
   Which jobs are they?

MAKING A SHELTER

When deciding where to shelter for the night you must look around you for suitable places and for materials you could use. You might find a cave or a hollow tree to shelter in, but it might be necessary to build your own shelter. Look around you to see what materials are available. If you are in a wood or forest, use branches of trees to form the basic shape of the shelter. You will need to tie them together, but what will you use for string? What if you don't have any string in your survival kit? What would you use instead? How do you make your shelter waterproof? Find out on this page.

SURVIVAL SKILLS WORK

For your shelter you collect lengths of wood. You need many pieces of wood, of several different lengths. You measure the branches you collect in centimetres, but your friend measures them in metres.

Your pieces of wood

210cm	232cm	495cm	500cm
180cm	181cm	255cm	505cm
550cm	320cm	195cm	50cm

Your friend's pieces of wood

0.5m	5.5m	1.81m	2.55m
5m	2.32m	2.1m	4.95m
1.95m	3.2m	5.05m	1.8m

Match pieces of wood that are the same length, like this: 210cm and 2.1m

CHALLENGE QUESTIONS

Use your answers to the survival skills work.
1) Put the lengths of wood in order of size, starting with the shortest.
2) Round each of the lengths of wood to the nearest metre.

(You will find a TIP to help you with this question on page 28)

SHELTER FACTS

Where you build a shelter is very important. It will depend on where you are:
- in the jungle you need to build your shelter off the ground to avoid creepy crawlies and snakes
- in the Arctic you need to build a shelter under the surface to protect yourself from the wind
- in the desert you need to build a shelter not to keep you warm, but to keep you out of the baking sun.

MAKING A SHELTER

1) First check the site you have chosen — is it free from dangers such as falling branches or likely flooding? Also avoid areas that have lots of animal tracks.

2) Clear the area and plan your shelter carefully. You don't want to make adjustments later. For example, the wind should not blow straight into the shelter's opening.

3) Select a long thick stick to go between two trees. Tie it to the trees using string or roots.

4) Place thinner sticks against the long stick to act as rafters. These should be long enough to form a shelter you can lie in comfortably.

5) Weave even thinner sticks in and out to make the framework rigid.

6) Now cover the shelter. Use bracken, ferns, leaves and pine branches. The covering should be about one metre deep. Don't forget to block the ends off so that you keep the wind out.

7) You can lay some logs on the ground for a bed. Cover them with the same material as your thatching.

8) Light a fire next to your shelter to keep you warm.

Making the frame of a shelter.

MAKING A FIRE

One of the most important skills for survival is knowing how to light a fire. Fire provides warmth and light at night. Most wild animals are frightened of fire, so lighting a campfire will make your shelter safer. You can use fire to boil water, which is often necessary for making sure that it is safe to drink. Food can be cooked on the fire, enabling you to have warm, safe food to eat. Lighting a fire will give a cold, tired group a **morale** boost, and the smoke may be noticed by rescuers. Fire is one of the most useful features for survival and, so make sure you always have matches on you!

SURVIVAL SKILLS WORK

Here are some pictures of different fires each with a circle of rocks around them.
Each stone measures 12.5 cm from end to end at its widest point.

$\bigcirc$ =12.5 cm

A

B
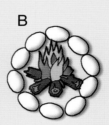

C

D

Can you work out the approximate **perimeter** of each fire? Give your answer in centimetres.
(The perimeter is the distance around the edge of the shape)

(You will find a TIP to help you with this question on page 28)

SURVIVAL FACTS

The outer bark of the birch tree makes good **tinder**. It can be peeled off and will light from a spark.

If a fire is built in a pyramid it is hotter and is good for a young fire, but when you want to cook you need to make the sticks flatter to provide an even heat.

LIGHTING A FIRE

1) Collect leaves, bark (birch is very good) and tiny twigs. This is your tinder. If it is damp, put the tinder in your pocket to make sure it dries out.

2) Break very thin dead twigs off trees and bushes and put them in a pile. Then collect a pile of bigger twigs (about the size of pencils).

3) Make two more piles, one of larger sticks and one of logs.

4) Decide the site for the the fire. Make sure it is not near low over-hanging branches. Dig a hole about 15 cm deep and about 30 cm in diameter.

5) Place green sticks in the bottom of the hole. They will keep the tinder off the damp ground and help the fire burn.

6) Set light to your tinder using a **firesteel**, matches or lighter.

7) When there is a strong flame, place the thinnest twigs on the fire. When they are alight, place the next thinnest on in a pyramid shape and so on.

8) Place smooth round rocks (about the size of a grapefruit) around the fire. This will stop the fire from spreading.

9) When you have a strong fire and a bed of embers, you can cook on the hot rocks.

CHALLENGE QUESTIONS

While you are all sitting around the fire you begin carving small pieces of wood. This is called whittling. Here are some of the shapes you have made.

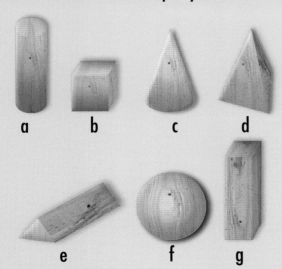

a   b   c   d

e   f   g

1) Name each of the shapes.
2) Which of them are types of **prisms**?
3) State how many **faces**, **vertices** and **edges** each shape has.

O nce you have sorted out a shelter, your next priority is to find a source of water. Without water or other liquid to drink, your body normally can only survive for 72 hours. But finding water when trying to survive is not always easy. Your group is lucky: you have found a fast-flowing stream and you can boil the water to make it safe to drink. As your group waits for the water to boil, you discuss other methods of collecting water. Everybody has a different idea of what to do. Some methods can only be used in sunny weather, others need rain or boggy ground. You all agree it is best to take enough water with you in the first place!

SURVIVAL SKILLS WORK

You talk about how much water you might collect if you use the different methods shown in the DATA BOX on page 19.

1) Find how much water you would have collected in total. Give you answer in millilitres (ml).
2) Is this more or less than one litre?
3) Most health organisations say you should drink between 1½ and 2½ litres of water every day. Have you collected the daily amount needed for one adult?
4) If an adult drank 1½ litres every day, how many litres would they drink in one week?

(You will find a TIP to help you with this question on page 29)

CHALLENGE QUESTION

You have two containers. One holds 3 litres of water. The other holds 5 litres.

How would you measure exactly 1 litre of water using both containers? You are not allowed to half-fill the containers.

(You will find a TIP to help you with this question on page 29)

DATA BOX   FINDING WATER

Your group discusses four different methods that you can use to collect water.

METHOD 1
Tie a cloth around your ankles and walk through a dew covered field. Squeeze water out of the cloths.
Water collected: 125 ml

METHOD 2
Dig into marshy or boggy ground. Use leaves and bark to scoop out water from the puddle.
Water collected: 55 ml

METHOD 3
On a hot, sunny day, tie clear plastic bags around leafy green twigs. Water will collect at the bottom of the bag.
Water collected: 275 ml

METHOD 4
Collect rain water by tilting your shelter and letting the water run into a **billy can**.
Water collected: 955 ml

If you are looking for a stream, remember that water travels down hill.

MOUNTAIN FACTS

Water boils at lower temperatures the higher you go. Near the top of Mount Everest, you can wash in boiling water.

People can live for up to 60 days without food, so finding food is not usually a top survival priority. However, one of your friends is feeling ill. You think he may feel better if he eats something. Nearby are some mushrooms that you can't identify. You leave them, because you know it is better not to eat anything unless you are sure it is harmless. Some mushrooms are so poisonous they can kill you. What other food can you find that is safe to eat? You find some berries, and as you look harder you begin to find all sorts of things to eat. Perhaps you wouldn't choose them to eat at a restaurant but they will keep you alive!

SURVIVAL SKILLS WORK

In the DATA BOX on page 21 you will see a **pictogram** that shows how many **edible** berries, roots, nuts, leaves, bugs and flowers you found.

Use the pictogram to help you answer these questions:
a) Which type of food did you find most of?
b) Which type of food did you find least of?
c) How many flowers did you find?
d) How many roots did you find?
e) How many more leaves than berries did you find?
f) How many more bugs than nuts did you find?

(You will find a TIP to help you with these questions on page 29)

FOOD FACTS

Don't be put off eating unusual items by the thought of the taste. Did you know:
• Earthworms taste like bacon rind.
• Fish eyes contain fresh water and taste like fried egg yolks.
• Ant larvae taste like shrimp.

CHALLENGE QUESTION

Look at the pictogram again. How many items of food did you find in total?

DATA BOX FOOD THAT CAN BE COLLECTED

A pictogram of the different edible food items that you found

Berries

Roots

Nuts

Leaves

Bugs

Flowers

KEY
= 12 items   = 12 items
= 12 items   = 12 items
= 12 items   = 12 items

CROSSING A RIVER

You and your friends survive the night, successfully lighting a fire, collecting safe drinking water and finding something to eat. As dawn breaks you decide that you must head for the bridge across the river. After several kilometres you reach Wobbly Bridge. Unfortunately 'Wobbly' is not quite the word for this bridge – since it has completely collapsed and fallen into the river. All that remains are a few pieces of wood on one side of the bank. You know you have to get across the river but one of your friends cannot swim. How will you all get to the other side without getting swept away or drowning? The answer is to use the pieces of bridge to make a raft.

SURVIVAL SKILLS WORK

You successfully make a raft but discover that only 2 people can travel on it at a time.

One person must always be on the raft or it will float away down the river.
What is the smallest number of times the raft will need to cross the river to get 4 people to the other side?

(You will find a TIP to help you with this question on page 29)

RAFT FACTS

A raft will keep you dry as you cross the river. If you swim you will get cold and wet. It may be difficult for you to get warm again, which could be dangerous.

Rafts are best for travelling along a river rather than just crossing one.

When you cross a river, keep glancing up the stream to make sure you don't get hit by anything being washed down stream.

TO BUILD A RAFT

1) Find 6-8 straight trees that are at least 3 metres long and about 20cm in diameter.

2) Cut them down, remove any branches so that you just have the trunks and lie them side by side.

3) If you have rope you can tie them together, but you can use tree roots or young branches. Tie the trees together at each end. Make sure that they are tied together well.

4) Carve a paddle with your axe or you could use a long stick like a gondolier.

5) Push the raft into the water and check that it floats.

6) Get on it (prepare to get wet, your weight at one end may make it go a little under the water). You should try to kneel rather than stand or sit until you are confident on the raft. Then either paddle or punt your way to where you want to go.

CHALLENGE QUESTION

It takes one person 8 minutes to cross the river. With two people on board, both paddling, it takes 6 minutes.

Look at your answer to the Survival Skills Work. How long will it take for the entire group to cross the river?

As your group heads on to the village that marks the end of your trip, you talk about the dangers and difficulties that you have faced. You were cold, thirsty and hungry, but you solved all of these problems. You built a shelter and lit a fire to keep you warm, you found water, and you gathered safe things to eat. You even managed to build a raft and cross a river safely. Your success was due in part because you were aware of the dangers and knew how to avoid them. What other dangers might you face during the rest of your trip? You and your friends come up with a list – some are more likely than others!

SURVIVAL SKILLS WORK

You talk to your friends about what dangers you might encounter. You think some dangers are more likely to occur than others. To be sure which dangers to be most alert for, you talk about the likelihood of each happening.

The probabilities are given here:

a) Get stuck in sinking sand	⅓
b) Get very cold (**hypothermia**)	⅚
c) Get struck by lightning	⅙
d) Bridge collapsing	½
e) Get eaten by a tiger	0
f) Get bitten by a snake	⅓
g) Fall climbing a cliff	½
h) Cut yourself with a knife	⅔

Probabilities can be shown on a **probability** scale from 0 (impossible) to 1 (certain). Mark the probabilities of each danger on this scale.

(You will find TIPS to help you with these questions on page 29)

SURVIVAL ADVICE

- Keep an eye out for tracks of dangerous animals.
- Look for areas where leaves have been disturbed. They might be covering a trap.
- In the jungle, always tread on logs when you cross over them. You don't know if there are snakes waiting for you on the other side.
- If you walk into **sinking sands**, don't panic. Take off any rucksack and lie on your back. Very slowly try to swim backstroke to the side.
- Look for the shape of human feet and boots. They can lead you back to civilization.
- Use all your senses, danger comes in many forms.
- If you have to leave your camp, leave a note or signs of where you have gone.
- If lost, walk down hill. Water travels down hill so you should come to a stream. Follow the stream until you get to a river. Follow the river until you get the sea. If you haven't found a village by then, turn left or right until you get to houses.
- When you get into a survival situation, make a plan and stick to it.

CHALLENGE QUESTION

'Impossible', 'Very unlikely', 'Unlikely', 'Even chance', 'Likely', 'Very likely', 'Certain'

Use words from the list above to say the probability of each of these events happening:
a) It will rain this week
b) The sun will rise tomorrow
c) A person in your family will be eaten by a wolf today
d) The day after Monday will be Friday
e) A new-born baby will be a boy

SIGNALLING

You are in sight of the village where you planned to end your trip. Unfortunately, as you cross some rough ground, your friend slips and twists her ankle. She's not too badly hurt, but she can't walk any further. You need medical help, but how do you find it? This is an area where you can't get a signal on your mobiles. Your decide to split up: the rest of the group will walk on to the village to get help, and you will wait with your friend. As you sit together, you talk about what you'd do if it had been just the two of you. You would have needed to signal for help. Do you know the Morse code for SOS?

SURVIVAL SKILLS WORK

In the DATA BOX on page 27 you will see the international Morse code.

1) If you used a whistle to spell out the message 'SOS' how many times would you blow the whistle? How many short blasts would you give and how many long blasts?

2) Look at the following messages:
   a) Come quickly
   b) Injured child
   c) Broken leg
   How many times would you blow the whistle for each message?
   How many short blasts would you give and how many long blasts?

*Small planes flying over remote areas carry **smoke flares** for signalling in an emergency.*

CHALLENGE QUESTION

The International signal for distress is six long blasts on a whistle every minute or six flashes with a torch every minute.
If you signaled with a whistle for 45 minutes, how many times would you blow the whistle?

(You will find a TIP to help you with these questions on page 29)

DISTRESS SIGNALS

If you do not have a whistle or a torch, you will have to use other methods to attract attention.

1) If you have lit a fire you could use smoke to get attention. Smoke can be different colours — black smoke is made from burning rubber and white smoke from burning green branches or leaves. It is important to think about which colour of smoke would show up best against the background. If you are in the desert, use black smoke. If you are in a forest, use white smoke. It will show up better against the dark trees.

2) Use something brightly coloured clothing to signal with. Wave a jacket, or (to signal to a plane) spread it out on the ground. Try to get up high to be seen more easily.

3) A mirror can be used to reflect the sunlight. Moving the mirror can make the light flash.

DATA BOX   USING THE MORSE CODE

Morse code is a way of sending messages using short and long sounds.
A short sound is written as a dot like this: •
A long sound is written as a dash like this: ▬
This is the international Morse code.

A • ▬	J • ▬ ▬ ▬	S • • •	0 ▬ ▬ ▬ ▬ ▬
B ▬ • • •	K ▬ • ▬	T ▬	1 • ▬ ▬ ▬ ▬
C ▬ • ▬ •	L • ▬ • •	U • • ▬	2 • • ▬ ▬ ▬
D ▬ • •	M ▬ ▬	V • • • ▬	3 • • • ▬ ▬
E •	N ▬ •	W • ▬ ▬	4 • • • • ▬
F • • ▬ •	O ▬ ▬ ▬	X ▬ • • ▬	5 • • • • •
G ▬ ▬ •	P • ▬ ▬ •	Y ▬ • ▬ ▬	6 ▬ • • • •
H • • • •	Q ▬ ▬ • ▬	Z ▬ ▬ • •	7 ▬ ▬ • • •
I • •	R • ▬ •		8 ▬ ▬ ▬ • •
			9 ▬ ▬ ▬ ▬ •

TIPS FOR MATHS SUCCESS

PAGES 6-7

Adding small numbers:
When adding small numbers you can add them in any order. Look for pairs of numbers that add to make 10 *such as 1 + 9, 2 + 8, 3 + 7, 4 + 6 and 5 + 5.*

PAGES 8-9

Making turns and measuring angles:
An angle is a measure of turn. Angles are measured in degrees. The symbol for degrees is °. One whole turn (a complete revolution) is **360°**. A quarter turn is **90°**, or one right angle. There are four right angles in one whole turn.
Remember that half a right angle is **45°**.

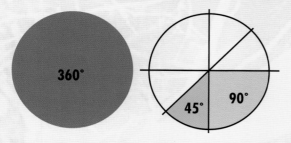

PAGES 10-11

Using coordinates:
To find the coordinates of a point on a grid, you read along the bottom of the grid first and then up the side.

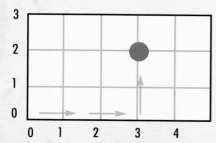

For example, a grid reference of **(3,2)** means **3 steps** along the bottom then **2 steps** up to find the exact point.

TIP: The phrase 'Along the corridor and up the stairs' can help you to remember this.

PAGES 12-13

Time measurements:
Remember that there are 60 minutes in one hour, 120 minutes in 2 hours, 180 minutes in 3 hours and 240 minutes in 4 hours.

PAGES 14-15

CHALLENGE QUESTION

Rounding numbers
Numbers ending in 5, 6, 7, 8 or 9 round up and numbers ending in 1, 2, 3, 4 round down.
So 1.4 metres would round down to 1 metre and 1.7 metres would round up to 2 metres.

PAGES 16-17

SURVIVAL SKILLS WORK
If you are finding 12.5 or 12½ times a number, halve the number first. Then multiply the number by 12 and add your two answers, e.g. to find 8 x 12.5
half of 8 = 4
8 x 12 = 96
then add your answers: 4 + 96
so 8 x 12.5 = 100

It might help you to know the numbers in the 12 times table

1 x 12 = 12	2 x 12 = 24
3 x 12 = 36	4 x 12 = 48
5 x 12 = 60	6 x 12 = 72
7 x 12 = 84	8 x 12 = 96
9 x 12 = 108	10 x 12 = 120

CHALLENGE QUESTION
Remember, a face is a flat surface of a solid shape. A vertex is its corner and an edge is the place where two faces meet.

  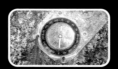  

PAGES 18–19

SURVIVAL SKILLS WORK

Remember that 1000 millilitres equals 1 litre.

CHALLENGE QUESTION

You can fill the 3 litre container and pour the water into the 5 litre container.
Now fill the 3 litre container up again.

PAGES 20–21

Pictograms:

A pictogram should always have a key to tell you what one picture stands for. Here each circle means 12 items, so half a circle stands for 6 items, one quarter stands for 3 items and three quarters stands for 9 items.

PAGES 22–23

SURVIVAL SKILLS WORK

Remember that one person must always bring the raft back across to pick up another person.

You might find it useful to draw out the crossings like this: ● = 1 person

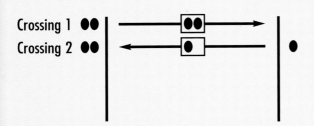

PAGES 24–25

Probability scale:

To show a probability you can mark a cross on the line. The cross on this line shows a probability that is likely to happen.

impossible   certain

ANSWERS ANSWERS ANSWERS

PAGES 6–7

SURVIVAL SKILLS WORK

Kit 2 is the best. It is worth 38 points.
Kit 1 = 34 points, kit 3 = 30 points, kit 4 = 36 points.

CHALLENGE QUESTION

One kit has all the items except the knife and the billy can.
The other kit could have either of these sets of items:
• knife, saw, firesteel, billy can and first aid kit
• knife, saw, firesteel, axe and sleeping bag

PAGES 8–9

SURVIVAL SKILLS WORK

1) a) S   b) E   c) NW   d) W

2) a) 45°   b) 135°

3) a) 135°   b) 225°

CHALLENGE QUESTIONS

1) Flat rock
2) Flat rock
3) the electricity pylon

PAGES 10–11

SURVIVAL SKILLS WORK

1) a) (-2, 2)   2) a) Soggy Swamp
    b) (0, 3)   b) Lone Tree
    c) (-1, -1)   c) Crumbling Cliff

CHALLENGE QUESTION

a) Soggy Swamp
b) Ling Marsh
c) Wooden Bridge

PAGES 12–13

SURVIVAL SKILLS WORK

The most useful tasks to do within the time limit are: building a shelter and lighting a fire. These jobs would take you 200 minutes (3 hours and 20 minutes), leaving you with 40 minutes to spare.

CHALLENGE QUESTIONS

1) a) 680 minutes   b) 11 hours and 20 minutes
2) Hunt for food and look for water

PAGES 14–15

50 cm	0.5 m	→ 1m
180 cm	1.8 m	→ 2m
181 cm	1.81 m	→ 2m
195 cm	1.95 m	→ 2m
210 cm	2.1 m	→ 2m
232 cm	2.32 m	→ 2m
255 cm	2.55 m	→ 3m
320 cm	3.2 m	→ 3m
495 cm	4.95 m	→ 5m
500 cm	5 m	→ 5m
505 cm	5.05 m	→ 5m
550 cm	5.5 m	→ 6m

PAGES 16–17

SURVIVAL SKILLS WORK

Fire A 112.5cm   Fire C 162.5cm
Fire B 125cm   Fire D 175cm

CHALLENGE QUESTIONS

1) a cylinder   e triangular prism
   b cube   f sphere
   c cone   g cuboid (rectangular prism)
   d triangular-shaped
      pyramid or tetrahedron
2) The shapes a, b, e and g are prisms
3)

shape	faces	vertices	edges
a	3	0	2
b	6	8	12
c	2	1	1
d	4	4	6
e	5	6	9
f	1	0	0
g	6	8	12

ANSWERS ANSWERS ANSWERS

SURVIVAL SKILLS WORK

1) 1410ml
2) This is more than 1 litre. It is 1.41 litres.
3) no
4) 10½ litres or 10.5 litres

CHALLENGE QUESTION

Fill the 3 litre container and pour the water into the 5 litre container. Fill the 3 litre container again and use it to fill the rest of 5 litre container to the top. This will leave you with 1 litre left in the 3 litre container.

SURVIVAL SKILLS WORK

a) leaves   d) 18
b) nuts   e) 6
c) 33   f) 30

CHALLENGE QUESTION

177

SURVIVAL SKILLS WORK

5 crossings   ● = 1 person

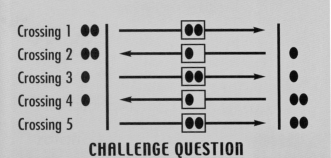

Crossing 1
Crossing 2
Crossing 3
Crossing 4
Crossing 5

CHALLENGE QUESTION

34 minutes

SURVIVAL SKILLS WORK

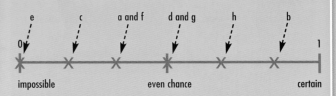

CHALLENGE QUESTION

a) Your answer will be Very unlikely, Unlikely, Likely or Very likely – depending on where you live!
b) Certain
c) Very unlikely
d) Impossible
e) Even chance

SURVIVAL SKILLS WORK

1) 9 times: 6 short blasts and 3 long blasts

2)

Come quickly	34 times	15 short blasts	19 long blasts
Injured child	35 times	24 short blasts	11 long blasts
Broken leg	24 times	13 short blasts	11 long blasts

CHALLENGE QUESTION

270 times

GLOSSARY

ANTICLOCKWISE The opposite direction from the way the hands of a watch turn round.

BILLY CAN A metal pot used as a cup or for cooking on a fire.

COMPASS A tool for helping you navigate. It usually shows the 8 compass points: North, North-East, East, South-East, South, South-West, West and North-West. Usually abbreviated as N, NE, E, SE, S, SW, W and NW.

EDIBLE Safe to eat, not poisonous.

FIRESTEEL A tool that can be used to create sparks to light a fire. You scrape the striker down the rod and it produces sparks at about 3000 °C.

GEOGRAPHIC NORTH The direction of the north pole. Maps show geogrphic north.

HYPOTHERMIA Where the body temperature drops and a person becomes very cold.

MAGNETIC NORTH The direction a compass points to. This is slightly different from geographic North.

MORALE The confidence and enthusiasm of a group.

NAVIGATION Finding your way.

NORTHERN HEMISPHERE The part of the earth that is north of the equator. For example Europe is in the Northern Hemisphere.

PROBABILITY How likely it is that something will happen.

PYLON A structure used for carrying power lines high above the earth.

PURIFYING Making clean. Water is purified to make it safe to drink.

SEMAPHORE A signaling system where two flags are held in different ways to stand for each letter of the alphabet.

SINKING SAND Deep wet sand sometimes known as 'quicksand'. If you get stuck in it you can sink lower and lower and can get buried.

SOUTHERN HEMISPHERE The part of the earth that is south of the equator. For example Australia is in the Southern Hemisphere.

SMOKE FLARES A cannister that can produce lots of brightly coloured smoke as a signal.

TINDER Small pieces of wood used to help light a fire.

MATHS GLOSSARY

ANGLE A measure of turn.

CLOCKWISE To make a turn in the direction that the hands of a clock move. Anti-clockwise is to make a turn in the opposite direction.

COORDINATES Two numbers in brackets used to show position on a grid, such as (3, 2) which means 3 steps to the right and 2 up starting from (0, 0).

DEGREES The units used for measuring angle °, or temperature °C.

EDGE A line that joins two faces of a solid shape.

FACE The flat surface of a solid shape.

FRACTIONS Made when shapes or numbers are cut into equal parts.

PERIMETER The distance all the way around the edge of a shape.

PICTOGRAM A chart where a picture is used to stand for several units.

PRISM A solid shape that is the same shape and size all along its length. If you slice through a prism parallel to its end face, the cut faces will all be the same size and shape as the end faces.

VERTEX (Plural VERTICES) A corner of a solid shape.

Picture Credits

Dave Tyler: 1, 4-5, 6-7, 8-9, 14-15, 18-19; Jonny Crockett 6, 15, 22-23; Mayang Murni Adnin: 20-21;
Free Nature Pictures: 10-11; Dynamic Graphics Group/IT Stock Free/Alamy: 26-27; Fotosearch: 24-25

Every effort has been made to trace the copyright holders, and we apologize in advance for any unintentional omissions.
We would be pleased to insert the appropriate acknowledgements in any subsequent edition of this publication.